DAY BY DAY

Affirmations for Moving Through Grief with Grace

grieve. grow. glow.

Kimberli A. Gross, M.A.

Dedicated to you, the reader.

Take what you need from these pages.
Let the words meet you where you are.

There is no right day to begin — only today.

Begin where you are.
Grace will meet you here.

A Note from the Author

If you're holding this book, there's a good chance you've been through something that changed you.

Loss has a way of doing that. It rearranges things — your sense of safety, your expectations, your identity. Sometimes it's loud and obvious. Other times it's quiet, lingering in ways you can't quite explain.

This book isn't here to rush you past grief or convince you to "move on." Grief doesn't work like that. And honestly, neither does healing.

What I do believe — deeply — is that grief and growth can exist at the same time.

I know this because I've lived it.

It has been over twenty years since my mother passed. I still have moments of sadness. Certain days still feel tender. But my life is no longer defined by loss alone. Over time, I learned how to live again — not by erasing grief, but by learning how to carry it with honesty, support, and grace.

That's what this book is meant to offer you.

Each week, you'll find an affirmation paired with a gentle challenge or reflection. Some weeks will feel validating. Others may push you to look at patterns, boundaries, or truths you've avoided. Both matter. Healing isn't only about comfort — it's also about courage.

There is no right pace here. No perfect way to use this book. You may move slowly. You may revisit certain weeks. You may feel resistance, relief, or something in between. All of it is welcome. This is not about becoming who you were before loss.

It's about becoming who you are now — wiser, more grounded, more honest, and more capable of joy than you may realize.

Grief may linger.
But so does grace.

And little by little, with intention and care, you can grow into a life that holds both.

Kimberli

Affirmation:

I am learning to settle into
who I am today
without rushing myself to
be anything more or less.

Pause for one minute today and take three slow breaths,
reminding yourself:

*"I am here.
I am safe enough to begin."*

Affirmation:

I give myself permission
to feel what I feel
without apology,
judgment, or fear.

Identify one emotion today and name it gently.

Allow it to be present without
trying to fix it.

Affirmation:

I honor my small steps.
Even when they feel quiet
or unnoticed, they still
count as movement.

Notice one small win this week – even if it's

*getting out of bed, eating well,
or resting with intention.*

Affirmation:

I am becoming more
aware of myself: my
needs, my limits, and
my capacity.

- 🌱 What felt hardest for me this month?
- 🌱 What helped me feel grounded or supported?
- 🌱 What did I learn about myself?
- 🌱 How did God show up?
- 🌱 One intention for next month.

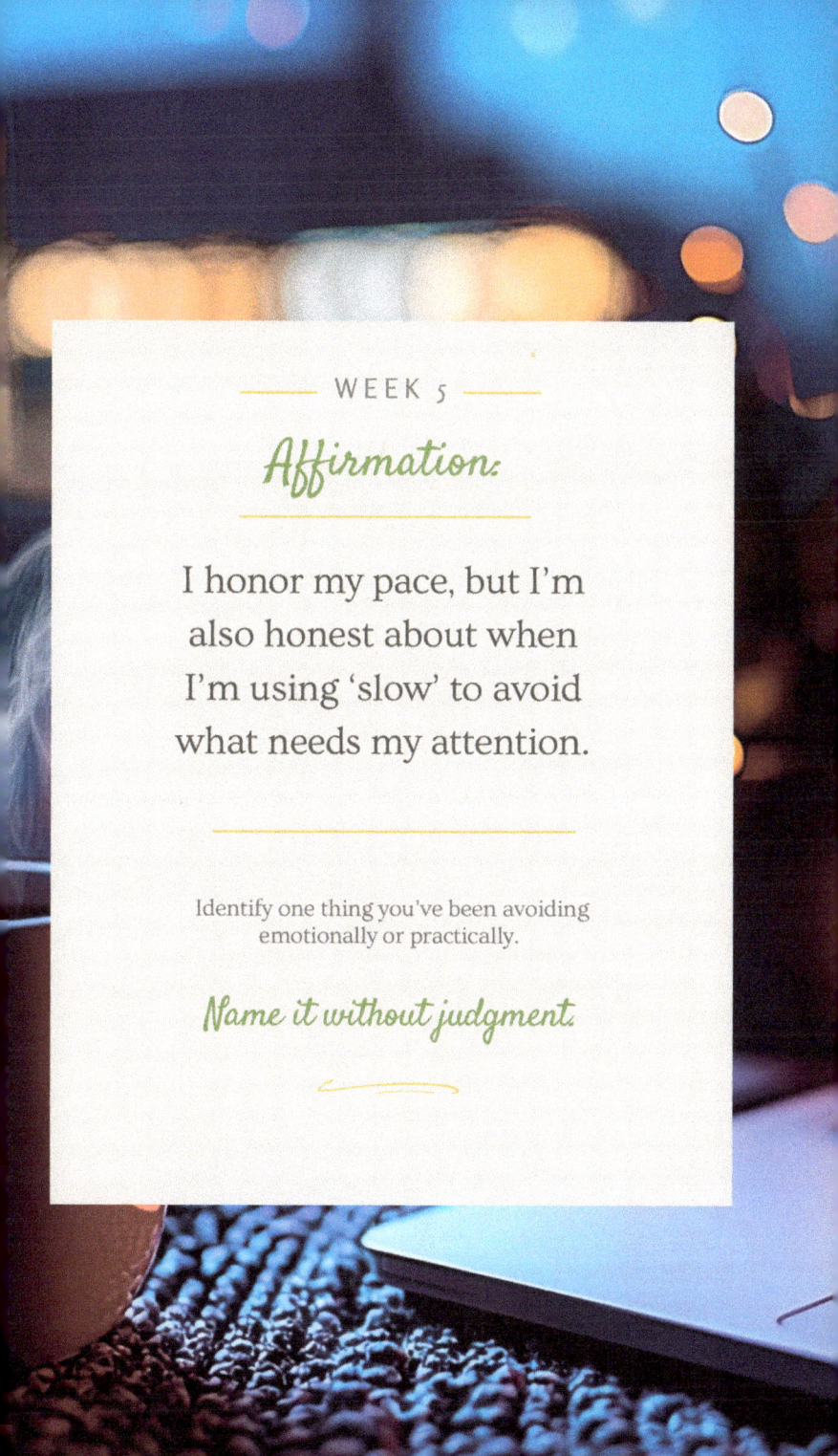

Affirmation:

I honor my pace, but I'm also honest about when I'm using 'slow' to avoid what needs my attention.

Identify one thing you've been avoiding emotionally or practically.

Name it without judgment.

Affirmation:

I allow myself to be seen
in my truth — not just the
polished parts, but the
real parts that need care.

Share one honest feeling with
someone safe this week.

Don't shrink it down.

WEEK 7

Affirmation:

I am capable of choosing
what heals me, even when
it's harder than what
temporarily comforts me.

Choose one healing action over one
numbing habit —

even for a moment.

Affirmation:

I'm learning to face myself with honesty and grace. Avoidance is information, not failure.

- What patterns of avoidance showed up?
- What truth am I dodging?
- Where did I show courage?
- How is God inviting growth?
- One uncomfortable step for next month.

I am honest about what
drains me, and I'm brave
enough to admit when I've
allowed behaviors or people
to take more than I can give.

Identify one draining pattern — internal or
external — and

say it out loud.

Affirmation:

I no longer shrink myself
to make others
comfortable. My healing
requires me to take up
rightful space.

Speak up once this week where you'd
normally stay silent —

even if your voice shakes.

Affirmation:

I own my part in my
healing without
taking responsibility
for what was never
mine to carry.

Reflect on one situation where you've
carried unnecessary guilt.

Release the guilt,
keep the lesson.

Affirmation:

I am reclaiming
power by learning my
patterns – not
judging them.

- Which patterns surprised me?
- Where have I given away power?
- What does taking up space look like?
- How did I show maturity?
- One boundary for next month.

Affirmation:

I refuse to keep repeating
stories that no longer
match who I'm becoming.
I am allowed to rewrite
the parts that limited me.

Identify one old story about yourself that
no longer serves you.

Looking Back, Gently

The first weeks of grief often ask one simple thing of us: to show up.
Not with answers. Not with strength. Just with honesty.
As you look back over these weeks, notice what may have shifted
— even slightly. Growth in grief is rarely loud. Sometimes it looks
like awareness. Sometimes it looks like rest. Sometimes it looks
like naming what you feel without judgment.
This isn't about measuring progress.
It's about noticing yourself.

Take A Moment

- What words or affirmations stayed with me?
- Where did I feel resistance, and what might that be telling me?
- What feels different now than when I began?
- What do I need more of as I continue forward?

With Grace

Affirmation:

I take responsibility for
my healing, not because
it's easy, but because I
deserve a life that mirrors
my growth.

Name one area where you've been waiting
for someone else to

fix what you can change.

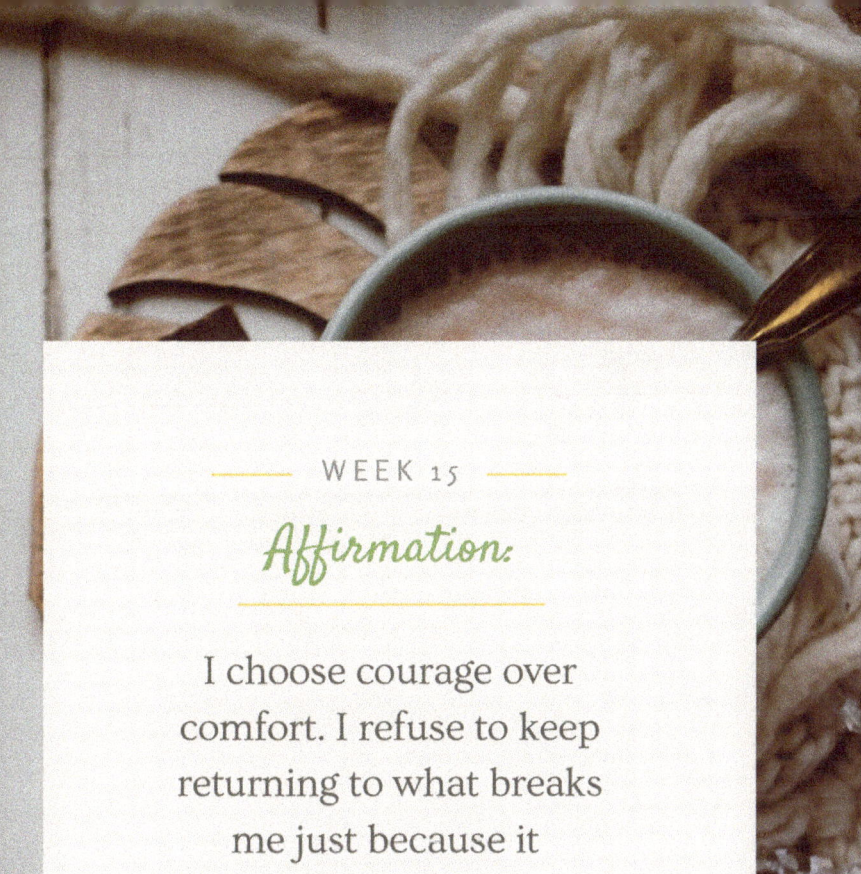

Affirmation:

I choose courage over
comfort. I refuse to keep
returning to what breaks
me just because it
feels familiar.

Take one step that disrupts a familiar but
unhealthy pattern.

WEEK 16

Affirmation:

I am becoming stronger by releasing what no longer aligns with the person I'm growing into.

❧ What limiting beliefs still grip me?
❧ Where did I choose comfort over courage?
❧ What truth did I face?
❧ What am I ready to put down?

Affirmation:

I am done abandoning
myself to meet
expectations I never
agreed to in the
first place.

Say "no" to one draining thing this week --
without apology.

Affirmation:

I deserve relationships
that honor my
humanity, not just my
strength.

Notice one moment where your needs
show up.

Don't dismiss it.

Affirmation:

Accepting support is not weakness. I am worthy of care, comfort, and compassion — without performing strength.

Ask for help once this week,

even if it's small.

Affirmation:

I am learning to show up
for myself and allow others
to show up for me —
without shrinking, hiding,
or overcompensating.

🌱 Where did I abandon myself?
🌱 What relationship patterns surfaced?
🌱 Where did I allow or resist support?
🌱 How is grief shaping my connections?
🌱 One relational boundary for next month.

Affirmation:

I am learning to respond
with intention instead of
reacting from old
wounds. My peace is
worth the pause.

When you feel triggered, take one deep
breath before responding.

Affirmation:

I no longer negotiate
with habits that have
proven they cannot
support the person
I'm becoming.

Identify one habit working against your healing.

Do the opposite once this week.

WEEK 23

Affirmation:

I trust myself to face
hard truths and make
hard choices. I can do
difficult things without
falling apart.

Choose one task or conversation you've
been avoiding and

take one step toward it.

Affirmation:

I am becoming a person whose actions match my intentions. Even my smallest choices can honor my healing.

- Where did I react instead of respond?
- What habits no longer fit?
- Where did I show resilience?
- What hard thing did I face?
- One pattern to interrupt next month.

Affirmation:

I am stepping into who
I'm becoming without
shrinking to fit the
expectations of who I
used to be.

Do one thing this week that reflects who
you're becoming —

not who you were.

— WEEK 26 —

Affirmation:

I am rebuilding my confidence piece by piece, and I no longer apologize for growing stronger.

Identify one area where you feel yourself improving.

Name it and own it.

Noticing What's Emerging

By now, grief may feel different than it did at the beginning. Not easier — just different. You may notice moments of steadiness, clarity, or curiosity returning. You may also notice new layers surfacing as you grow.

This season often brings a shift from surviving to noticing. Patterns may become clearer. Needs may feel easier to name. The questions may change — from How do I get through this? to How do I want to live with what I've lost?

Growth here doesn't require certainty.
It asks for honesty and self-trust.

Take A Moment

- What themes or affirmations have resurfaced?
- Where have I noticed greater awareness or clarity?
- What boundaries or needs am I beginning to name?
- What feels like it needs more care right now?

With Grace

WEEK 27

Affirmation:

I release shame that was
placed on me by
moments, people, or
seasons that never knew
my whole story.

Write down one shame-based belief
you're letting go of — then

speak a counter-truth out loud.

Affirmation:

I am learning that joy
doesn't erase my pain; it
expands my capacity to
live fully.

Where did confidence show up?
What did I release?
How did I make space for joy?
What relationship grew stronger?
What do I want to expand next month?

WEEK 29

Affirmation:

I trust the wisdom within
me. I am learning to listen
to my inner voice instead of
silencing myself for the
comfort of others.

Make one decision based solely on
what *you* know

is right for you.

Affirmation:

I am building emotional stability by honoring my limits, managing my energy, and not forcing myself beyond my capacity.

Identify one limit you need to honor this week —

and follow through.

Affirmation:

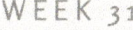

I no longer abandon my
needs, silence my truth,
or shrink my standards
just to feel included.

Notice one moment where you're tempted
to minimize yourself.

Choose alignment instead.

Affirmation:

I am learning to be
someone I can rely on —
emotionally, spiritually,
and mentally.

🌱 Where did I trust myself?
🌱 Where did I betray myself?
🌱 What pulled me out of alignment?
🌱 What boundaries protected my peace?
🌱 What does stability look like right now?

Affirmation:

I am not guilty for feeling
joy. Joy does not erase
my grief — it expands my
capacity to live fully.

Notice one moment of lightness
this week.

Acknowledge it.

WEEK 34

Affirmation:

I release the pressure to
compare my healing to
anyone else's. My
journey is sacred and
unfolds at my pace.

Identify one area where comparison steals
your peace.

Refocus on your lane.

Affirmation:

I am capable of starting
again. I am not bound to
who I was in seasons
of pain.

Name one new beginning you're willing
to open yourself to.

Affirmation:

I am becoming someone
who can hold joy, grief,
hope, and truth at the
same time.

❧ Where did joy surprise me?
❧ What am I learning about maturity?
❧ Where did comparison show up?
❧ What new beginning am I walking toward?
❧ How am I different from six months ago?

Affirmation:

I am growing into
someone I can be proud
of – not perfect, but
present, intentional,
and honest.

Identify one way you've shown growth in
the last three months.

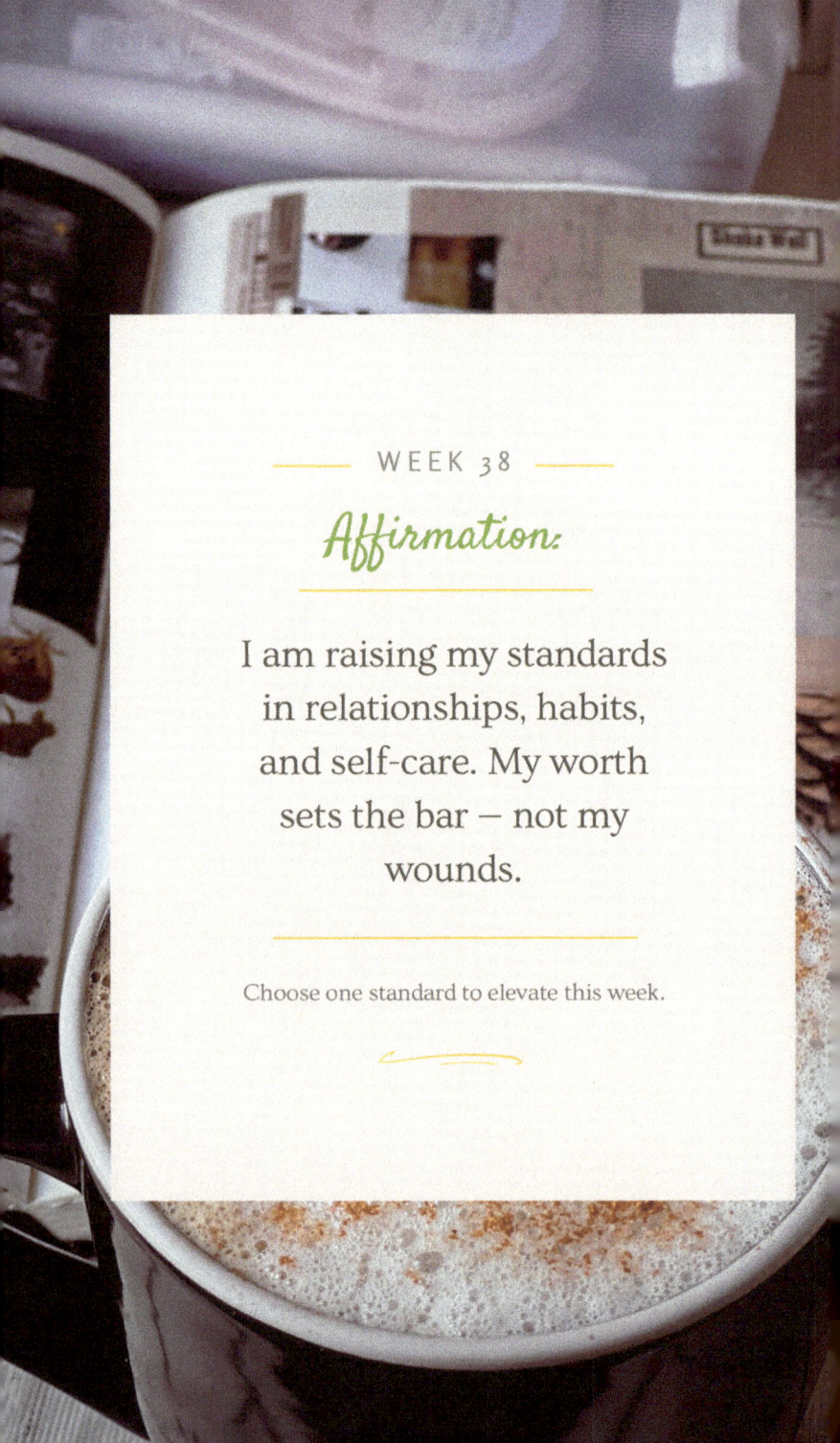

WEEK 38

Affirmation:

I am raising my standards in relationships, habits, and self-care. My worth sets the bar — not my wounds.

Choose one standard to elevate this week.

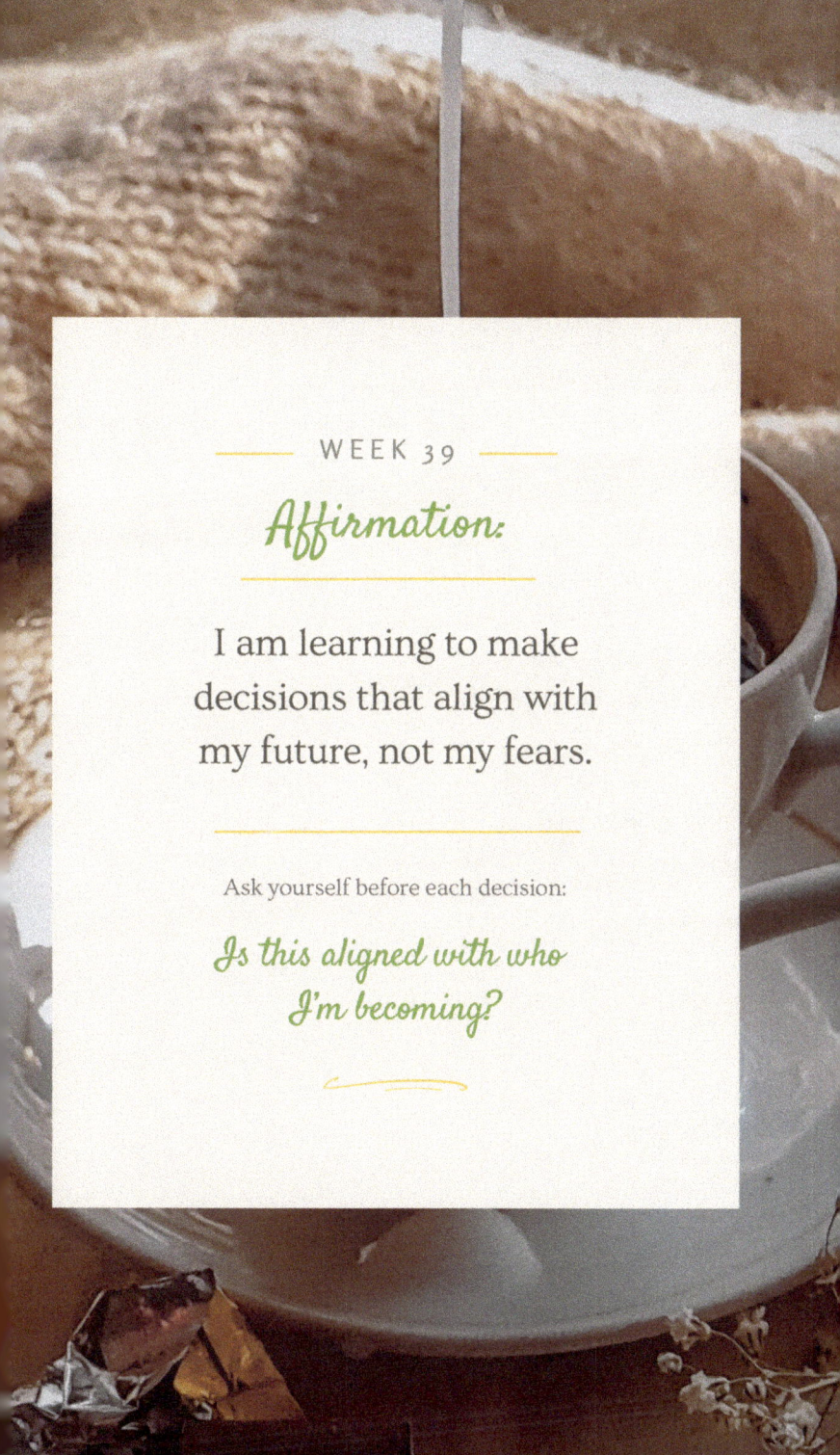

———— WEEK 39 ————

Affirmation:

I am learning to make
decisions that align with
my future, not my fears.

Ask yourself before each decision:

*Is this aligned with who
I'm becoming?*

Living With What You Carry

GGrief may no longer sit at the center of every moment — but it hasn't disappeared. Instead, it may be woven into how you see yourself and move through the world.

This season often brings quiet questions of identity:
Who am I now? What matters most? What am I carrying forward — and what am I ready to release?

Living forward doesn't mean leaving grief behind. It means learning how to carry it alongside meaning, connection, and care.

This is not a return to who you were before loss.
It is an unfolding into who you are becoming.

Take A Moment

- How has my understanding of myself shifted?
- What feels essential to carry forward?
- What no longer fits the life I am building?
- Where do I sense alignment in how I'm living?

With Grace

Affirmation:

I am outgrowing patterns,
people, and expectations
that do not honor who I
am becoming.

❧ What no longer fits me?
❧ What relationships feel misaligned?
❧ Where did I show integrity?
❧ What did I refuse to settle for?
❧ What am I releasing moving forward?

WEEK 41

Affirmation:

I no longer chase chaos out
of habit. I choose peace, even
when it feels unfamiliar.

Identify one area where you've been
choosing chaos.

Step back from it.

WEEK 42

Affirmation:

I stop carrying emotional
burdens that were never
mine to hold.

Notice one burden you've been carrying
for someone else.

Release it.

Affirmation:

I am no longer defined
by the version of myself
that existed in
survival mode.

Write one sentence describing

who you are now.

Affirmation:

I am stepping into a
version of myself shaped
by truth, courage, and
grace — not trauma.

What peace did I practice?
What burdens did I release?
What version of myself am I shedding?
Who am I becoming?
How have I matured?

Affirmation:

I honor the strength it took to get here. My journey deserves to be acknowledged.

Name three ways you've grown this year.

Release it.

WEEK 46

Affirmation:

I am learning to live from
intention instead of pressure,
guilt, or obligation.

Say one intentional 'yes' or 'no' this week

from a place of clarity.

Affirmation:

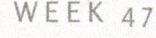

I trust my ability to lead
myself — in decisions,
relationships, healing,
and hope.

Do one thing this week that reflects

emotional leadership.

Affirmation.

I am preparing to step into a new season with clarity, strength, and gratitude.

❧ What strengths surfaced?
❧ What intentional choices did I make?
❧ Where did confidence show up?
❧ What am I most grateful for?
❧ What am I carrying into my next chapter?

Affirmation:

I believe there is more for
me — more joy, more
purpose, more life than the
pain I've survived.

Write down one thing you are expecting

in the next year.

Affirmation:

I am no longer guided
by fear. I choose purpose,
even when the path
is unfamiliar.

Identify an area where fear is loud.

Decide your purpose-driven response.

WEEK 51

Affirmation:

I am ready for what
comes next. I step
forward with
confidence.

Name one courageous step you'll take

in the next 30 days.

Affirmation:

I enter this new season
whole – not because life
is perfect, but because
I've learned to carry truth,
joy, and healing together.

❧ Who am I now?
❧ What did I overcome?
❧ What strengths did I discover?
❧ What vision do I hold?
❧ What promise am I making to myself?

Holding It All

As you reach the end of this year, you may notice how much you've learned — not because grief disappeared, but because you stayed present with it.

What once felt overwhelming may now feel more familiar. Not lighter, necessarily — but held with greater care and understanding.

This season invites integration. It asks how grief, grace, growth, and joy can exist together. Healing isn't an ending; it's an ongoing relationship with your life as it is now.

This work doesn't conclude here.
It continues — day by day.

Take A Moment

- How has my relationship with grief changed?
- Where do I see evidence of grace in my life?
- What truths or practices do I want to carry forward?
- How do I want to continue living — with intention and care?

With Grace

Returning to These Affirmations

You may find yourself coming back to these affirmations long after you reach the final week.

Grief isn't something we complete — it's something we learn how to live with. Different seasons may call for different words. An affirmation that once felt distant may later feel grounding. One that felt comforting early on may eventually challenge you in new ways.

You don't need to start over or follow a specific order. You can return to the weeks that resonate most, revisit affirmations during difficult seasons, or sit with one page for as long as you need.

This book is meant to meet you where you are — again and again.

Take A Moment

- What feels more familiar or less frightening than it once did?
- What have I learned about myself through this season?
- What helps me stay grounded when grief resurfaces?
- What does living with grace look like for me now?

This book can meet you again whenever you need it.

With Grace

With Grace

With Grace

With Grace

With Grace

With Grace

About the Author

Kimberli A. Gross, M.A. is the Founder and CEO of Celebrate Still, LLC., a grief support and education organization dedicated to helping individuals and families learn how to live fully after loss.

With a Master's degree in Human Services Counseling and a focus on trauma, crisis response, and grief support, Kimberli brings both professional training and lived experience to her work. Her approach is grounded, compassionate, and honest — centered on the belief that grief does not disappear, but growth, grace, and joy can exist alongside it.

Through workshops, support groups, coaching, and guided resources, Kimberli helps others build a new normal rooted in self-trust, resilience, and hope. Her work creates space for grief without rushing healing and encourages forward movement without erasing love.

grieve. grow. glow. reflects both her personal journey and her professional mission: to walk with others as they learn how to carry grief — and still live.

For workshops, speaking engagements, or facilitated group experiences, email **info@celebratestill.org** or visit www.celebratestill.org.

Stay Connected: @celebratestill (Facebook & Instagram)